Camdean School

HEALTHY TEETH

Constance Milburn

Wayland

Healthy Living

Healthy Teeth
Healthy Hair
Healthy Skin
Healthy Eyes
Healthy Hands and Feet
Healthy Eating

Words printed in **bold** are explained in the glossary

First published in 1990 by
Wayland (Publishers) Limited
61 Western Road, Hove
East Sussex, BN3 IJD, England

Reading consultant: Diana Bentley
University of Reading
Editor: Rosemary Ashley

British Library Cataloguing in Publication Data
Milburn, Constance
   Healthy teeth.
   1. Man. Teeth. Development and care
   I. Title II. Series
   612'.311

   ISBN 1–85210–902–5

Typeset by Rachel Gibbs, Wayland
Printed and bound in Belgium
by Casterman S.A.

Contents

Why we want healthy teeth

Look at these smiling children. They look good
because they all have strong, healthy teeth.

4

We need our teeth for biting and chewing food. Without teeth we wouldn't be able to enjoy a crunchy apple or a packet of crisps.

Teeth are important to us when we speak, too. If we have any teeth missing we may not be able to speak clearly.

Different types of teeth

We grow two sets of teeth. The first set are called milk teeth and we have 20 of these. When we are about six years old our milk teeth start to become loose and fall out. That's when we have funny gaps in our front teeth which sometimes makes it quite difficult to speak clearly.

Then we grow a second set of teeth. These are permanent teeth and we have them all our lives.

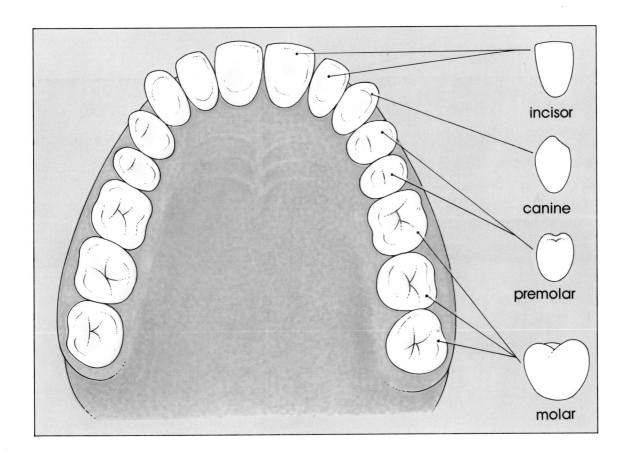

incisor

canine

premolar

molar

Our front teeth are called **incisors**. They are for cutting. The teeth at the back are called **premolars** and **molars**. They are for grinding and chewing. In between the incisors and molars are the **canines**. **Canines** are slightly pointed. They are for cutting and tearing.

We usually get four more teeth called **wisdom teeth** when we are grown up. Altogether we should have 32 permanent teeth.

Growing healthy teeth

Teeth are made of a substance called **dentine**. The dentine is covered with a hard coating of **enamel** for protection.

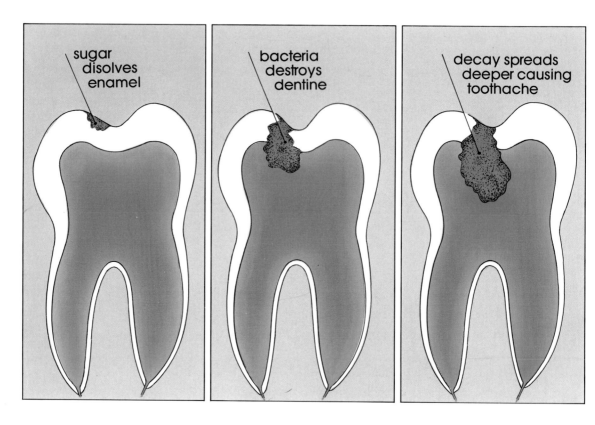

sugar disolves enamel

bacteria destroys dentine

decay spreads deeper causing toothache

To grow healthy teeth we need to eat the right food. We especially need two substances called calcium and **fluoride**. Calcium is needed for dentine to form. Fluoride is needed for the layer of enamel to form.

Calcium is found in: milk
                       cheese
                       cereals
                       vegetables
                       meat
                       fish

Fluoride is found in: most tap water
                       certain toothpastes
                       fish

How teeth go bad

We all like to eat sweet things. But too much sugar can cause teeth to go bad or decay. This is because tiny germs called **bacteria** live in our mouths. They feed on the sugar that we eat. This forms **acid**. Sugar added to the germs and acid in our mouths forms a sticky layer called **plaque**.

Plaque builds up between the teeth and sticks to them where they meet the gums. The acid in plaque softens the enamel covering our teeth and they begin to decay.

Plaque is not easy to see because it has no colour. If plaque stays for long on the teeth it forms a hard layer called **tartar**. This then has to be scraped off by the dentist.

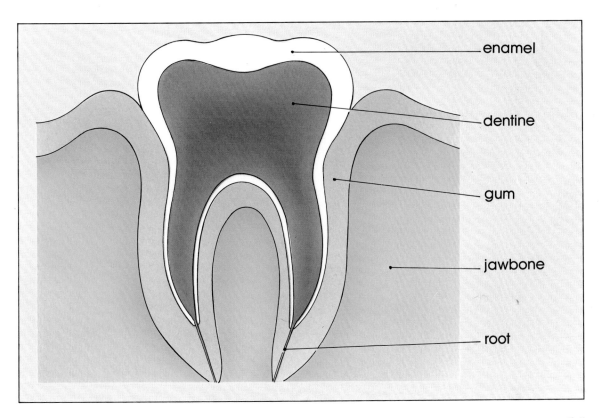

enamel

dentine

gum

jawbone

root

Keeping our gums healthy

It is very important to make sure our gums are strong and healthy. Sore, swollen gums can cause our breath to smell nasty. They can also cause our teeth to become loose and even fall out.

The best way to make sure our gums stay healthy is to eat plenty of fresh fruit and vegetables. **Vitamin C** is essential for keeping our gums strong and healthy. Citrus fruits, such as oranges, lemons and grapefruits, blackcurrants and green vegetables all contain vitamin C.

Plaque causes gum disease as well as tooth decay. It builds up on teeth just above the gums, and can cause them to become swollen and sore. So it is doubly important to make sure that plaque does not form on our teeth.

Keeping our teeth strong

Here are some of the best ways to keep teeth healthy and strong.

- Brush teeth after meals, especially after breakfast and before going to bed.
- Use a soft toothbrush which is in good condition. Old, bent bristles will not brush out the food and they could damage your gums.

- Use toothpaste that contains fluoride. Fluoride helps to prevent tooth decay. After brushing your teeth, swill your mouth out with water.

- Visit the dentist every six months. The dentist can stop tooth decay quickly.
- Eat plenty of raw vegetables, fresh fruit, cheese, fish and meat. Drink plenty of milk.

- Do not eat too many sweet things. When you do eat anything sweet, make sure that you clean your teeth afterwards.

Good and bad habits

These are good habits:
- Eating fruit instead of sweets. Fresh fruit is good for teeth and the natural sugar in fruit will not harm them.
- Nibbling sticks of carrot and celery when you feel hungry. Raw vegetables help to make teeth strong.
- Drinking natural fruit juice with no added sugar.
- Eating nuts, seeds and dried fruits such as raisins and sultanas instead of sweets.
- Always cleaning teeth after eating.

16

These are bad habits:

- Sucking lollipops, chewing sticky toffees, eating sweets and chocolates.
- Drinking sweet fruit squashes and fizzy drinks.
- Adding sugar to cups of tea, coffee and other sweet milky drinks.
- Eating sweet biscuits and cakes between meals.
- Forgetting to clean teeth after meals and before going to bed.

How to be sure our teeth are clean

We know about the damage that can be caused by plaque. And we know that plaque is not easy to see because it is colourless. But there is a way to see if all the plaque has been brushed off our teeth. Ask the dentist for some **disclosing tablets**.

Chewing one of these tablets will make parts of your teeth turn pinky red. Try one and see!

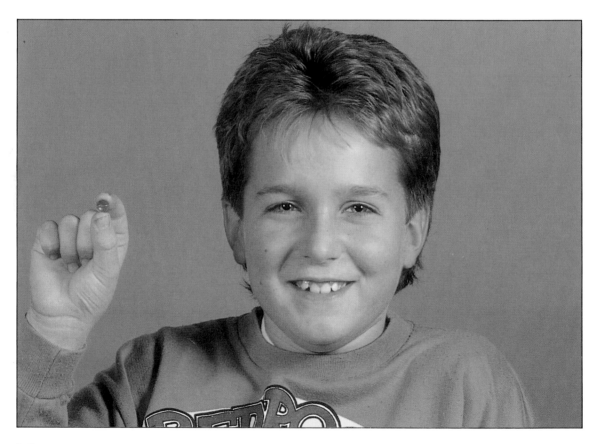

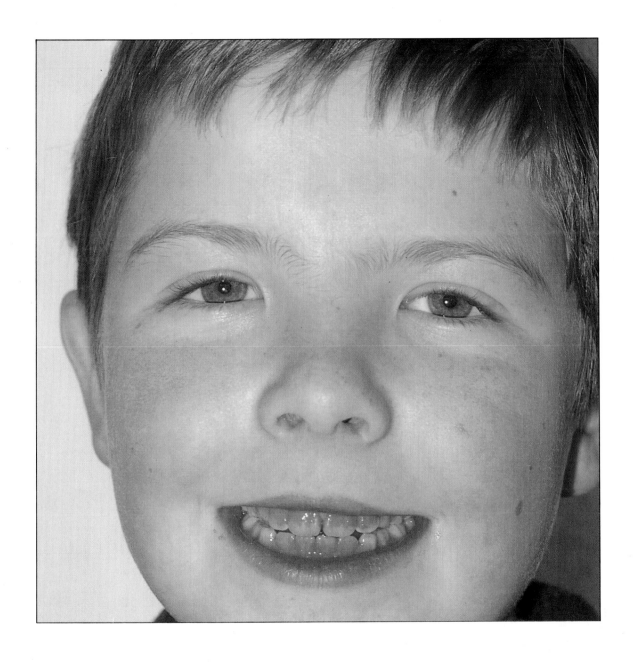

If you look in the mirror you will have a surprise. The pink spots show where the plaque is sticking to the teeth. So brush them again and clean off all the plaque.

Brushing and cleaning teeth

The best way to keep teeth clean is by regular and careful brushing.

- Put some toothpaste onto your toothbrush.

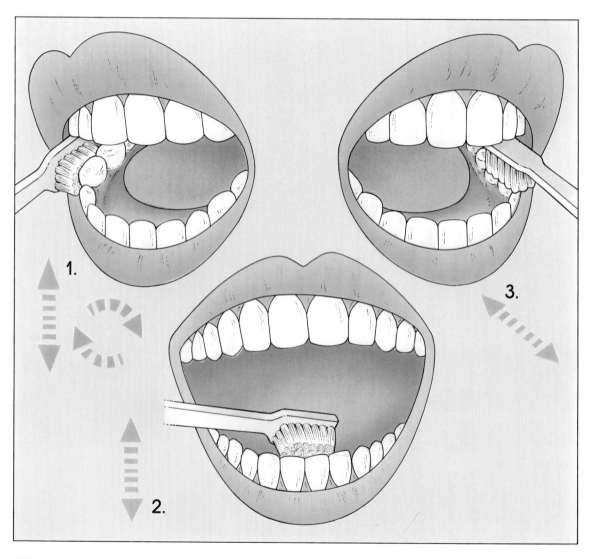

- Brush up and down and round and round in small circles. (1.)
- Open your mouth wide and brush the inner sides of your teeth. (2.)
- Brush the biting and chewing surfaces too. (3.)
- Swill your mouth out with water.

Brushing will not always clean between teeth that are very close together. To get rid of food that is stuck between your teeth you need to use **dental floss**.

Pull the floss gently down between your teeth and scrape it up and down the side of each tooth.

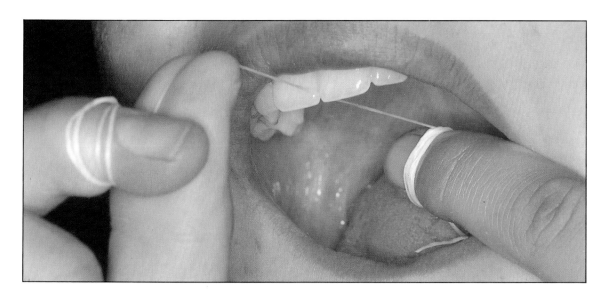

Work all round your mouth with the floss and then rinse out with clean water.

Visiting the dentist

When you go for a check-up the dentist will look carefully at each tooth. The dentist uses a special small mirror to look behind the teeth.

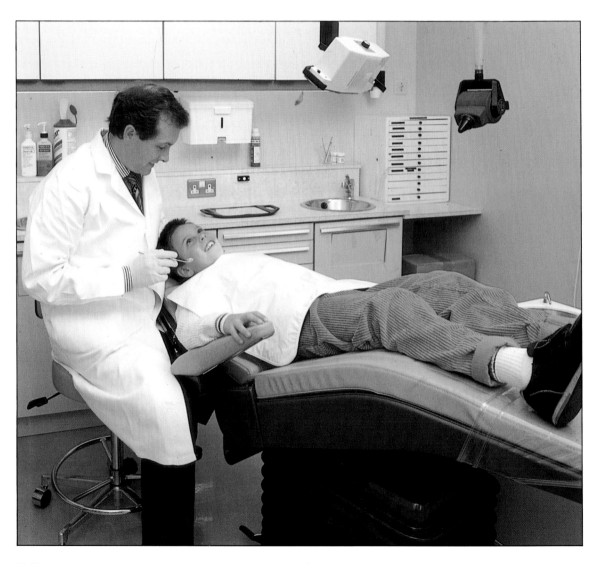

If there is nothing wrong with any of the teeth the dentist may polish them with a small, round brush. Afterwards the teeth will feel smooth and clean.

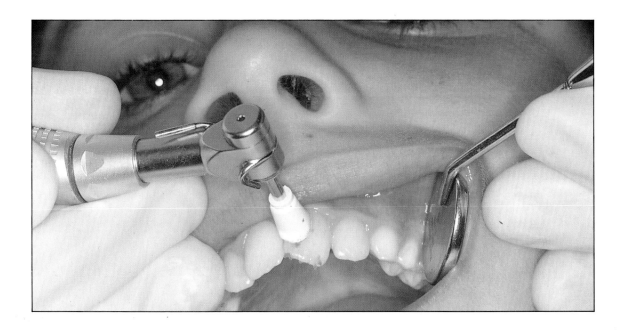

Seeing the dentist every six months makes good sense. You may also need to see the **hygienist**, who will make sure your gums are healthy.

The dentist will fill any holes before they become too big. Having a small filling is much better than having a large one.

Large **cavities** can form in teeth without causing any pain. So even if you have no toothache, this doesn't necessarily mean that all is well with your teeth.

How the dentist treats a cavity

Acid in our mouths can cause a hole in the enamel coating of our teeth. If the hole reaches the dentine underneath the enamel the tooth may ache. Germs may get inside the tooth and the cavity will become larger. The tooth will need filling.

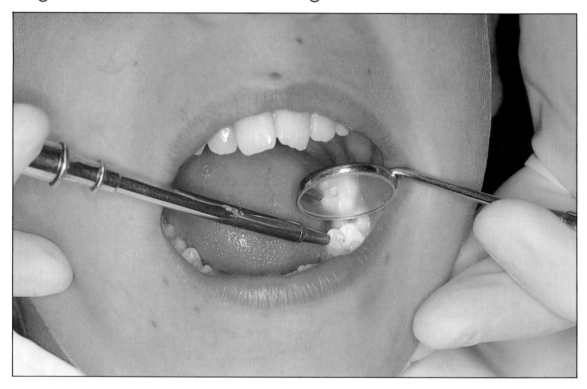

First the dentist may decide to **numb** the tooth and the gum before filling the tooth. This will stop any feeling of pain.

The dentist will drill out any decayed parts and fill the cavity with a special mixture called **amalgam**. When the hole is filled, the amalgam is smoothed off. Now there is no way for germs to get inside the tooth.

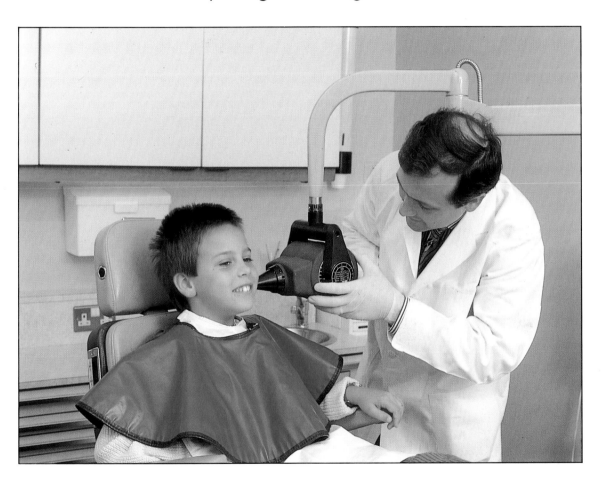

Sometimes the dentist will want to take an **X-ray**. This doesn't hurt at all and will show up any cavities that the dentist cannot see.

Crowning and straightening teeth

Teeth that are too decayed to be filled may be **crowned**. The dentist may file the tooth to make it smaller and then fix an artificial cap onto it with special cement. Crowns are also used to mend teeth that have been broken in accidents.

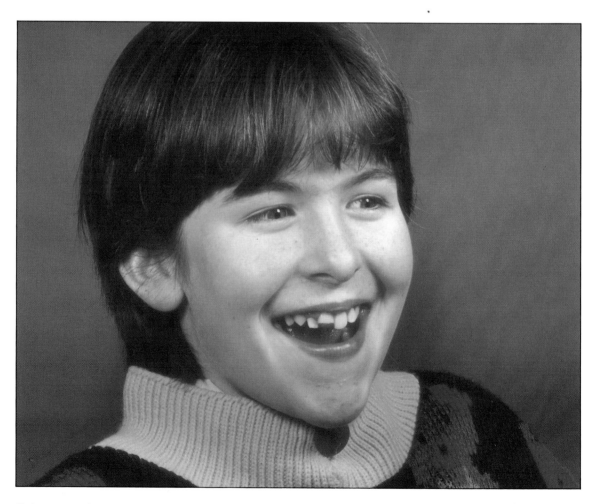

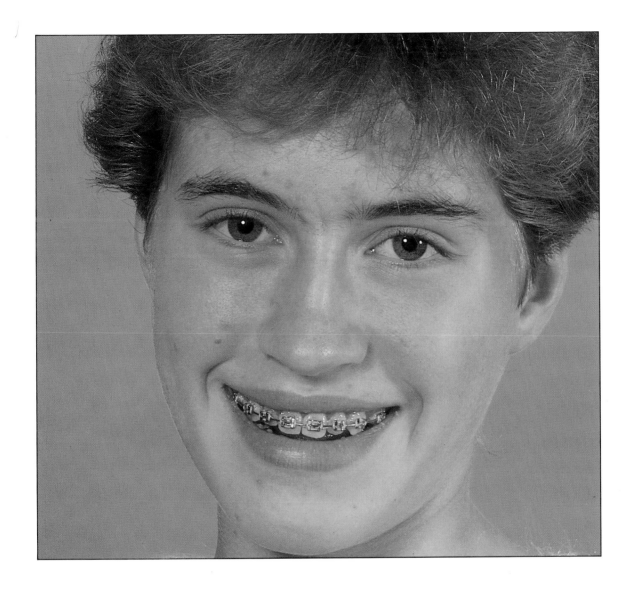

Sometimes teeth do not grow straight. The dentist can make a wire **brace** to straighten crooked teeth. This may not feel very comfortable at first but you soon get used to it. It will be well worth the slight discomfort because afterwards the teeth will be straight.

Healthy teeth for life

When our parents and grandparents were young it was quite usual for people to lose some of their teeth before they were very old. Sometimes they lost all their teeth.

They lost their teeth because they did not know the importance of eating the correct food. That is why some older people have false teeth.

We know now what we must do if we want to keep our teeth healthy. If we follow all the rules in this book we should have good, strong, healthy teeth all our lives.

Glossary

Acid A chemical substance that can destroy a hard surface.

Amalgam A mixture of metals used to fill teeth.

Bacteria Germs that can cause disease.

Brace A wire appliance which is fitted onto teeth to straighten them.

Calcium A substance that makes teeth strong.

Canines Pointed teeth.

Cavities Holes or hollows in a tooth.

Crown An artificial protective covering that is fixed to a damaged tooth.

Dental floss Waxy string used to clean between teeth that are close together.

Dentine The softer part of a tooth under the enamel.

Disclosing tablets Special tablets which show where plaque is sticking to teeth.

Enamel The hard white covering of a tooth.

Fluoride A chemical that helps to stop tooth decay.

Hygienist Someone who helps the dentist by making sure that teeth and gums are healthy.

Incisors Cutting teeth.

Molars Chewing teeth.

Numb To have no feeling.

Plaque A sticky layer of acid, bacteria and sugar.

Premolars Grinding and chewing teeth.

Tartar A hard, crusty deposit which forms on teeth.

Vitamin C A substance found particularly in citrus fruits and green vegetables that is essential for healthy gums.

Wisdom teeth The last four molars to grow.

X-ray A special photograph which shows the dentist if there is anything wrong inside a tooth.

Books to read

Body Facts by Dr Alan Maryon Davis (MacDonald, 1984)

Dental Care by Brian R. Ward (Franklin Watts, 1986)

Going to the Dentist by Kate Petty (Franklin Watts, 1989)

My Visit to the Dentist by Diana Bentley (Wayland, 1989)

Teeth by John Gaskin (Franklin Watts, 1984)

Your Teeth by Joan Iveson-Iveson (Wayland, 1985)

Index

Picture acknowledgements
All photographs are provided by Trevor Hill except for page 29,
which was supplied by Zefa. All artwork is by John Yates.